Parturition

Parturition

Heather Treseler

SOUTHWORD*editions*

First published in 2020
by Southword Editions
The Munster Literature Centre
Frank O'Connor House, 84 Douglas Street
Cork, Ireland

Set in Adobe Caslon 12pt

ISBN 978-1-905002-70-2

Contents

Louisiana Requiem

For Emily McMains

Eight months pregnant when your mother began hospice,
   you sat in the driveway, belly ovoid as an imperial Fabergé

egg on the eve of the Bolshevik Revolution, or so you joked
   with your dying mother whose love of metaphor shone

through the morphine fog and night air in Baton Rouge,
   thick with magnolia three days gone and the sweeter

tang of silverbell: fecund humid buzzing air a soft coverlet
   over your swollen limbs. You sat, mulling the bald

cypress trees older than your grandpa who made the old
   money selling insurance in the New South. A way,

he said, selling it, of investing in one's blood, one's kith
   and kin, the next generation, whatever the Lord saw

fit to happen. Money, firm as a pillared manse, this grand
   house turned *palliative*, which is to care for without

curing, cognate with *pall* and *pallbearer*, cloak and carrier
   of the coffin before earth's coverlet brings the body

home to its colder self. Just now, giving your mother water
   and hummed song, you cushion the earthward journey,

her accession to gravity, longing in aqueous eyes, turned
   inward and unseeing. All the while, the child inside

you assumes her own gravity, plotting descent, though her
   head is stuck stubbornly under your ribs, her feet locked

against the pelvic gate. To carry a child, to bear the borning,
first labor of the endless labors, to concede to the gravity

of love's body: those nights, sitting outside your mother's dying
room, warm earth pressed against the backs of your bare

legs, your hand running over knobbed ribs of cobblestones
your father set down, years ago, in some Roman fancy

of having a drive like the Appian Way: *timeless, enduring.*
There, in earshot of the night nurse, you let night

envelop you in its perfume, blended scent a pagan incense,
the worship of nature and of the moon, rounding like

the child inside you, dimpling its impervious face as you
pray for the pain to recede from your mother's body

and for the body, receding. And you are an entire country,
an America, stretched impossibly across a Mason Dixon

and two shores, nearing: the woman who bore you, daughter
you will bear, your body a hinge between its history

and future, an imperfect present tense. Scientist, dedicated
to cool notice of detailed fact, resistant to the muddled

logic of metaphor, you nonetheless find yourself borne
across by likeness in otherwise radical difference:

the shared violence that marks birth and death, mothering
the grade that governs the latitudes of the in-between.

Mother, no placid person or thing, but a rugged engine,
suing for peace: to bring forth a world from a fallen

world as a child from the long dark veins. Mother a river,
   inexhaustible as water; a song of warmth and warning;

a map for the body, politic; a long cobbled road, umbilical,
   built to outlast wreck and ruin, the death of empire.

Parturition

Low sounds of morning trains to the city woke
me with their soft metallic clacking, oars chapped

against water. Shock of a steady check and warm
apartment: one month in which mothering felt

possible. Bearing a child, or finding one in need
of a mother, with or without the adjunctive chaos

of a man or a woman, a mate with whom tides
of erotic fever, dissipation might occur alongside

rituals of care, the shared endeavor of raising
a responsible person: the project thought to be

natural to a couple or to the business of being
a woman. (Story I had been told for as long

as I knew I was supposed to have a story, telos
of girlhood its reproducibility, its end marked

by another's beginning.) Later, I'd recognize that
October hunger as bodily response to a pause

in want (steady check, warm apartment) as men
seek brothels after battle. My dream of a child

a reaction to surfeit, to harvest and a habitable
hovel that promised more than one safe winter.

Within weeks, it had vanished, that ghostly
infatuation. What they claimed was instinct

and part of nature, not a month's seduction.
Not a shotgun marriage of sprigged hope

and release from long exhaustion. I had read
a Roman historian who wrote of Athenians

made to oar triremes into war across the wide
bowl of the Aegean. Their nakedness whipped

by leather sun. The historian noted a phenomenon
—or had I dreamt it, falling asleep in the riddle

of an ablative absolute? Incidents of hoplites
reaching port who, allowed at last to stand,

filled with frenzy, strained to leap overboard.
Not, surmised the chronicler, in suicidal longing.

But as wasted arms stirred with hallucinatory
flight and salted wounds, carved like a runic

alphabet across their blistered backs, broke
freshly open as if the body were trying to sign

or to speak in its red ink. And the water
they had milled, hour after hour, no longer

seemed a torment but a mirror in which
they could see, in another like the self,

who they had been, and what (having won
a war) they had been made to surrender.

NULLIPARA

Since fruit trees, medlars and mulberries,
aren't the only arbors required
to sustain life as we have known it:
cherish more than your ravenous mouth.

SKYWALKER

Years after recovery, you encounter a sinewy woman
  in a Lacan seminar who can't shut up about desire,

drive, deferral, her eloquence a kind of death-flirting
  performance like Charles Blondin tightroping

across Niagara in a blindfold. You see the ropy veins
  in her hands and face; iliac crest visible through

corduroy pants; two shirts under a floral summer blouse;
  the bird's nest of chest bones: classic midlife disease.

Yet you listen intently, each week, drunk on the sherry
  of her florid speech that mimes tones of authority.

Voice, voice fishing beyond the body for a kind mammal
  or patch of land on which to breathe, shelter, stand.

You don't allow yourself, looking, to feel marvel or pity:
  your lack of envy a measure of health, though your

smugness at her suffering disgusts you. Not too long ago,
  you were the anorexic hiding out in blowsy clothes,

a war zone's barrack of bones. Looking at her, you recall
  what the old bearded Jungian half said, half sang

to you, insistently, in your worst year, "Wholeness,
  dear, not perfection," and how your addled ear

heard "holeness," siren song of negation more perfect
  to you than a body, even a baby's born without

flaw into the wild startle that must be air in virgin
  lungs. Your hard wish to slip appetite's nanny,

girlhood's noose, stride across the sky's broad stage,
  mouth's incessant gorge, sure in your mastery

of gravity, footing, lines strung above roaring water,
  as you angled to step beyond self and hunger.

Caul

You are six times more likely to be twice struck by lightning
    than born with an amniotic sac scarved about your head:

child of the veil, the old ones said, their Old World membranes
    broken, by necessity, in New Canaan. Born in caul, she is not

holy or haunted, not friend to prophets or ghosts inherited, but
    stirred by life's bright brashness, its carousel sights that beg

for sound: as on an afternoon in late October, the ocher light
    a famishing gold, a woman carries a harp across her back

and turns to face traffic, her profile like a Wyeth in an aqueous
    meadow in Maine. She bears the instrument of her making,

walks as if steered by its inaudible weight: what remains hidden
    in portage: the dearth before melody, the blind birth of song.

The Lucie Odes

For Lucie Nell Beaudet (1960-2018)

I.

I'd known you six years before you told me
how your first husband pimped you out—
used the cash to buy a fried chicken franchise

along a rural highway in Alabama. How you
slept under the counter where you cashiered
wings and thighs. How you rinsed, out back,

and spread baby powder across a bath towel
to soak up the tumid August sweat, keep off
skittering roaches. For the rest of your life

you had nothing to do with chicken. Mixed,
in memory, with the smell of strange men's
semen. How you dreaded what came despite

rough-shod precaution. How you stole from
the till, dollar at a time, until you had enough
for a bus to the clinic. I picture you there alone,

benumbed, draped and gauzed in a steel theater,
vowing never to seek what had been siphoned.
How, after, he hunted you with a shotgun

not to get you back but to put the narrow shape
of you under his dirty boot, under carmine soil.
He called you darling pay-dirt, his working girl,

and promised broken knees; a bullet in each
palm; a tongue ribboned; and your eyes gored—
in primitive backwoods punishment and burial.

II.

Twenty-seven bucks got you as far as St. Louis,
once the gambol of young Thomas Stearns Eliot,
an indoor creature, his double hernia delicately

trussed as he daydreamed his mahogany future
staring into the glass of Prufrock's Furniture,
plotting revenge against the failure of his flesh.

You heard, on the radio, that Eliot was the great
poet from St. Louis, so you bought his *Quartets*,
recited the liturgical lines as you washed floors

nightly at the medical school. There, you met
Dr. Fischer, famed neuroanatomist, fugitive
of Kristallnacht, who insisted on cleaning his

own lab to Wagner's *Flying Dutchman*. He saw
your mop and asked your name. Within a week,
you'd offered to work for free if he would train

you in pathology and to his surprise, you loved
perfusing tissue, fixing slides, teasing disease
into blooms of legible color. You did not flinch

at gutted cadavers or dank shit of euthanized
chimps. Neither of you spoke of a past, of men
mechanized in murder who killed off a sister,

or the dark knives in a drunk mother's slurry
kitchen. Both of you, schooled in subterfuge,
took temporary refuge in never looking back.

III.

Unlikely from the start: our friendship
in a night course where I felt a fraud,
teaching adults as old as my mother.

You with the cornflower blue eyes, silk
blouses, Chanel blush, and cat-eye glasses,
classing up the class. My ugly orthopedic

shoes and brace. Both of us learning to act
from half-wrecked bodies: my accident
a small occasion beside your catastrophe,

paralysis, metal chair. In your essays,
I learned of the reckless man who sped,
flipped his car, the chassis' shear of your

thoracic spine, a tailpipe's tattoo of your
long leg. How Dr. Fischer visited, daily,
as you recovered. I learned, too, of your

penchant for opera and Creole cooking,
Melville and Eliot. And of your technical
job, the spellbind that is mitosis: daughter

cells twinned in chromosomes, circumstance.
Ballet of mirror neurons. After the last class,
I walked to your car while snow squalled low

over the sullied city, Prufrock's retreats. Soon,
I was sidekick and kid sister. Two solitudes
opened to the field and furrow in each other.

IV.

What you knew: how to anesthetize a small
animal without it seeing the glint of needle.
Sculpt perfect blue lunettes and dark kohl

over the eyes; launder black lace; rise early
and stay up late; quell heartbreak, hangover.
Coax a cork or cactus bloom. Plump a soufflé,

dodge a bible thumper. That year, my petite
reckoning: a man-child to whom I'd been
betrothed called it off late one night, in a fit

of rage, as I lay down to sleep. For weeks,
I dozed upright in a shabby sublet where
the lights arced and fused, drunks caroused

in the alley, and silvery bats flew down from
the chimney. To you, I brought a draft horse
heart, its plodding illogic circling the empty

shape of its own yearning. Freud, we agreed,
had few things right. Not Rat Man or poor
Dora. But id and ego as horse, uneasy rider.

The armor of *amour-propre* donned, as adults,
learning self-regard as if by paint-by-number.
We talked Heidegger. Blared the Pogues while

the tabby cat hid in the closet, and we poured
each other nightcaps: two women, determined
not to fear living, the alphabetic rune of scars.

V.

At your table, *a slow rotation suggesting
permanence.* By day, the dining room
served as an atelier where I prodded

and patched sentences, anchored at dry
salvages. By night, the apartment turned
salon of scientists, poets, unlonely widows,

an Olympic gymnast, a wry phlebotomist,
a felon. After tiring days at the lab, you
alchemized a perfect evening, converting

ordinary time into occasion, the planned
luck of good company. Girlish, we hung
glass baubles from the chandelier, sat

Dr. Fischer's ashy cigar by the window,
leavened the politics with poems, long
workdays with wine. I laughed, there,

in spite of myself. Dared to kiss your
regal forehead. Served as line chef,
steering clear of your stovetop's merry

burble. When we were alone, flopped
in bed or driving through the city,
listening to *Aida* or *La Sonnambula,*

I felt cherished as comrade, confidante,
chérie. In our evident brokenness, love's
tacit fabric wove between us, incarnate.

VI.

By edict of will, you outlived the mother who
planted her Cadillac in the flowerbed, chrome
crushing the bougainvillea. Groans, then howls

from the bedroom where he locked her to sober
up. Mother, who baptized you good-for-nothing,
her great mistake, so when a slick-talking shyster

paid you mind, feeding crumbs to the gullible,
you gave in to his one-ring circus. Being wed,
then being whored—fleeing him, months later,

with the feral instinct of a woman suffering
unspeakable violation—you left with a clean
blouse and a clutch of dollars stuffed in Keds.

In the ballad of odd jobs, you trilled each note:
waitress and escort, nanny and janitor, card
shark and croupier. You sloughed off vestiges

of marriage, took on life as if it were jack
or backgammon. *Steady stakes, no prison or
religion*: your motto in those years. *No god,*

no hard time. And no looking back, though
you gave stern side-eye to each new reality:
how to avoid assault and battery; cauterize

a bleeding cervix; dodge a punch and charm
the paunchy; flatter the vain and indigently
wealthy; fire a flan; stay lean and healthy.

VII.

We dreamt of a love outside of proprietary
rights, the subtle tyranny in the habendum
clause, 'to have and to hold,' in the contracts

for land and slaves, water rights and wives.
Many women, you said, *don't realize they must
direct their fate. But if you are your own master*

—she stirred bouillon into the boiling pot—
*then there's no need to offer your body as daily
remittance for safety or children, the leisure*

*to love in a suburban kitchen, in a quaint town
with low crime rates, good schools. To live
without mortgaged desire, to husband your*

*own strength, to take or dismiss lovers from
your own sweet bed by the court and jury
of your own opinion, to have and to hold*

*your body without lien or claim, boot or bank
or another's name, to depend on no man—
take it from me kid, from this chrome chair,*

*habendum is freedom, that diamond-tipped
obsidian, that most feared thing: a woman's
mind without border, box, or ceiling. Measure*

*your loves by how they espouse your license
to live with nothing hid or hindered, halved,
withheld: largesse that never leaves you less.*

VIII.

To love another woman as if the self.
In your arms, sculpted from sculling
your lean body across each distance;

in your eyes' ready laugh; in the riddle
of a thin-lipped smile; in legs' vestige
of your walking days: a testament to

the beauty of metamorphosis. Love,
then, in the slight leeward list of ribs,
your delicate hand angled to mark

a point or tuck my wayward hair.
To love another woman, as much
as the self. When we found ourselves

in bed, breathless with champagne,
I wondered: how bright could I make
your eyes in this twilit room where,

by fiat, we deemed there was no other
law? After you were gone, I climbed
back into bed, soft nest of your hair,

the sheer splendor of warmed skin.
Old bed, where yearning pulled us
to anchor in the loam of each other;

soft bed, where we breathed, cleaved
together; high bed, by west window,
where, later, you curled and died.

IX.

Summer of young unarmed Michael Brown,
summer of massacre. Summer another white
man reckless with car and gun left a body

like offal, spread-eagle on asphalt, hot road
pressed against his unbearded face as he bled
from six wounds and a three-fifths clause.

What is ratified in acts of Missouri Compromise
and expedience: that old logic of 'nicety' in tidy
gated streets of Clayton, Frontenac, and Ladue

where feudal sacrifice of someone else's child
is a week of headline news, and county officers
exact salary and pension from carceral zip codes.

We watched the city dehisce along its veteran
scars; we drove in the heat to the little grocery
in Florissant where you found work, after your

accident, and learned to guide your chair down
aisles before returning to your lab's chemical
vials. Ferguson, where folks often offered

to help you, and East Saint Louis, gangrened
in poverty, quarantined by highway and high
rise, where you bought supplies, cheap leads

and catheters. We grieved as Brown was killed
in the street and again, in the news; we gathered
and mourned how it is we wound and wound.

X.

I got a job and left for good, relieved as young
Eliot to part from the murder and middling mud
of the Mississippi, its ritual riverbed unburials,

unsettled silt that clots at the heart. You had
promised to retire, settle your affairs, and join
me in New England in a house by the ocean.

(*How selfish, then and now, my love for you,*
oh woman more than mother or lover and both.)
Because there is no escape from the wheel,

no quota for how much one soul must freight,
infection began to roil in your unfeeling flank.
And I wasn't there to see you, naked. Too late,

surgeons chased its septic reach, coring deep
into bone. You forbade me at your bedside:
work and write, chérie; it isn't yet time for worry.

I begged. On the phone, your gulley laugh, old
smoker's warble, the balm of your voice reaching
from the morass you felt to be your sinking body.

The nurse assured me there was no sign of distress
or harm, your flesh still warm. Atheist, anarchic,
no barefoot Jesus on your horizon, you took one

last spin down Kingshighway where you stood,
where you strode from that steaming wreck:
leggy, lone, owning no one but yourself.

ANHEDONIA

What, now, to pair with bread? After you died,
I could not think of what to eat: riddling illogic

to every flavor, a revulsion to the idea of taste
or savor in the bitter winter after the coroner

ratified, with sterling knife, you hadn't meant
to die. 'No conclusive evidence of self-harm,'

his voice procedural, calm. Still, it seemed you
made a deliberate gift of the shriven sunken

lake of your bluing body, your mermaid legs
that had not moved for twenty years, the steel

rods that held your spine upright. Sacrifice,
pyre: when they slid you from table to fire,

giving you back to vapor and ash, flame took
the hennaed auburn hair where I had always

buried my face: your body, your bread pared
from me, unpaired. And I stood there naked,

raw for shelter: each woman's house built
on the long bones and breath of a mother.

Voyeur

From where I stood, holding my shoes,
  guarding the pile of clothes repealed
    from the summer of their bodies:

two women in their prime, a version
  of it that is (and isn't) about fecundity,
    rendering a life beyond the one given.

Three women, two nude, thawing from
  a New England winter so fierce it broke
    records, pipes, roof rakes, vertebrae,

grim cheer in local habits of hibernation.
  In the belated warmth of June, I tucked
    my feet in cooling sand. After a winter

wormed in dark, alone in the fish bucket
  of self, desire like a young nun's chafing
    under vow, like a colt's neck rubbed raw,

I was needful of touch or aqueous freedom,
  the cool of unguarded lake. They called,
    laughing nakedly in water, two women

swimming nearer to their summer, each
  of us wanting to break a law: the idiom
    of how our lives were spoken before

we uttered our names. I kept a lookout,
  fearing arrest of police or pleasure,
    though I'd sped them in the old

Honda, its pouting bumper sailing
   the highway to a kettle pond
      I imagined grateful for shapely

legs, brunette and blond, whirring
   beneath its surface. Two women's
      arms, sawing across dark water,

like Caillebotte's pair of barebacked
   laborers: bent, brute, lithe to cull
      old varnish, planing to raw wood.

WAGER

For you, I have left my clothes on the floor.
  I have left windows open in the bedroom.

We might scandalize the neighbors. We might
  entertain house painters. We might captivate

a stag line of squirrels on the telephone wire,
  watching what we do: touch both tender

and terrifying: naked fate in small furies of love.
  Pairs of fleshly doors that open to rapture or

metaphor: a chance to be momently carried across
  into somewhere, something, someone else.

WEATHER

A small rain down can rain but I am not outside, beside
an aluminum mouth of a gushing gutter, watching
the city sluiced in the casual event of falling water.

Nor am I standing in a shale of rubble, circled by dead
children's toys, or crouched in a buckling raft, crusted
in cold salt and urine, chattel in a game of rockets

and gas. I breathe from two lungs, integral, my legs
warm under blankets' nightly benediction. And love
lies sleeping, unharmed and unarmed beside me, arc

of his shoulder familiar as landscape to a painter whose
hands remember the curves of two cleaved hills, forelock
of treeline, wild mane of sky. I trace hollow shadows

in a dark naming of parts as if my lover were a getaway
horse: throatlatch, barrel, and cannon; pastern, gaskin,
and hock. Tender, the names given to boats and beasts

of burden, what carries us from port to ocean, trailhead
to highway, midnight to morning, censure to pleasure:
fugitives from dreamt disasters. My beloved of nape,

buttock, and thigh; or stern, winch, and turnbuckle; or
dock, loin, and withers: in your body's boat, I stow trust
for safe passage while distant wars make their incursions,

violence sends its newsworthy summons, and weather makes
a music of time. *A small rain down can rain* and by luck, Christ,
or zeitgeist, I cradle him in sleep's long sail toward morning.

SEABIRDS

And how they angle their bodies over water
with tensile intention, masters of hover
and swoop, dart and splay.

Technique in these storm petrels at the level
of instinct which, watching from shore, we
might mistake as pleasure,

claiming each elegant instance of nature
as something ultimately about ourselves,
not a good meal's necessary

murder, the calculus of want that drives
a beak's precision. In the foreshortened
days before solstice,

the business of sleep hardly put away before
we are, at midday, craving it again: a retreat
into warmth from the low

dark that comes over cape houses and marsh
in the startling cold of matchstick December
and the shirred mirror

of a half-frozen salt bay. We sat in a warm
car, watching the last hour of light ravish
then subtract itself from

the winded tapestry of reeds, the slick backs
of feeding petrels. We admit to envying
their honed vision,

their eyes' detection of the flicker of fin,
as known to them as a mate's plumage.
How have we arrived

at early mid-life to find desires opaque,
or dimmed to a decibel beyond hearing?
In the scripts that fell,

hidden mantles, on the children we once
were, in early grief of knowing we were
wrong, from the start,

unable to trust in the unseen; or to see without
seeing to the point of pain; to bear, willingly,
the brunt of family

ambition and name into regard if not renown.
To fear, even then, the ostracon of tribal shun
and to have shaped

a twinned existence, giving to Caesar in accord
with his remand, while hiding a spare and shiny
penny, bright as a bird's

eye, as our own. The petrels' theater is governed
by nature: they act in concert with belly and bone.
They are not otherwise,

abroad or at home, they do not shirk from violence
in algorithmic continuance. Their songs' necessity
a midwinter music.

Whatever is the opposite of keening, that is the sound
the waves make, trawling themselves across the long
shallow shore in Ogunquit, Maine: home, in another
century, to fishermen who built a tidewater basin,
furrowing the soft marshland, digging a channel
to give safe harbor to boats named "Susan Bee,"
"Clementine," and "Anna Mae." In time, shucking
shacks and sturdy docks sprung up in Perkins Cove,
with a drawbridge and coils of hemp rope weathered
like hands scored by clam knives and raw mornings
that redden the nose faster than whiskey or a woman
in heat. Fishermen, you imagine, lived by tides,
their ancient faces buffeted like driftwood cast
on the beach by the last spasm of storm.

Painters arrived later, drawn by the ubiquity of light,
the changeling shore, these clapboard houses jutting
like defiant chins from the bluffs, each built like
an axiom from Emerson: self-trust; innate spark;
nature's mirror of soul; each man a forgivable god.
Here, against the ocean's sotto voce, a gravelly drawl
like the history of smokes in a lounge singer's voice
urgent in its surges, slow in the pleasure of its retreat.
Here, overlooking a saltwater strand as if it were your
birth canal, the history of your angst and wailed arrival.
Here, alongside white sand and dark wet rocks that cover
it, lovingly, lending land some provisional protection:
solidity against the inquest of water, which is a version
of time, and warmth, though it be from stones.

Here, in a cliff-side cottage, you discover your lover's
unfathomably delicate ear, curved softly as a conch shell,
and the hewn channel of his pelvic girdle, its melding
of smooth muscle and bone almost feminine in its line,
though it hinges a man in his centaur existence half
above, half below a navel that buttoned him, once,
to the first woman to offer him hospitality, the care
of her body. That day, you found little to say, little
to squander in speech. For the first time, when you fell
back, sated, you didn't need to ask what he was thinking,
you didn't ransack the shelves for some abiding crumb
to feed lingering hunger; you had, for once, satisfied
what took you past girlhood's parish and garden gate,
granting exile permission and village, citizen and state.

Acknowledgements

"Louisiana Requiem," *Frontier Poetry*, Winner of the Frontier Poetry Summer Prize in 2018, selected by the editors of *Frontier Poetry*

"Parturition," *Notre Dame Review*

"Skywalker," *Cincinnati Review*

"Caul" and "Anhedonia," *Alaska Quarterly Review*

"The Lucie Odes," *Missouri Review*, Winner of the *Missouri Review*'s Jeffrey E. Smith Editors' Prize in 2019

"Voyeur in June," *The Worcester Review,* Winner of the Frank O'Hara Poetry Prize in 2016, selected by Henry Walters

"Wager" and "Seabirds," *Matter*

"Weather," *SWWIM*

> This poem adapts the second line from the anonymous sixteenth-century quatrain:
>
> > "O Western wind, when wilt thou blow
> > That the small rain down can rain?
> > Christ, that my love were in my arms
> > And I in my bed again!"

"Shorelines," *Crosswinds Poetry Journal*, Second Place in *Crosswinds Poetry Journal*'s annual contest, selected by Lloyd Schwartz

I am indebted to the late Michael Harper for his aegis and gentle insistence; to Anthony Walton for the impetus and sounding; and to the friendship and conversation of Nausheen Eusuf, Megan Marshall, Jahan Ramazani, Virginia Konchan, Lauren Alleyne, Kathleen Ossip, Jonathan Ellis, Sarah Giragosian, Amy Savage, Christina Davis, J. D. Scrimgeour, January Gill O'Neil, B. K. Fischer, Daniel Pritchard, Anna V. Q. Ross, Alyse Knorr, and Marvin Campbell.

I am also grateful for residencies and fellowship support from the T. S. Eliot House, the Brandeis Women's Studies Research Center, the Boston Athenaeum, the Virginia Center for the Creative Arts, and the American Academy of Arts and Sciences. The Worcester State University Foundation, President Barry Maloney, alumna Judith O'Connell Hoyer, and my colleagues Kristin Waters, Hank Theriault, Lisa Boehm, Matthew Ortoleva, Dennis Quinn, Don Vescio, and Karen Woods-Weierman all provided timely support and encouragement.

My thanks to my family; my family of dear friends; and the late Lucie Nell Beaudet.

www.ingramcontent.com/pod-product-compliance
Lightning Source LLC
Chambersburg PA
CBHW021946040426
42448CB00008B/1261